Table of Contents

Introduction – Life is Too Good for Bad Study	4
Superhabit 1 – The Power of an A+ Effort in Class	12
Superhabit 2 – The Power of Single-Tasking	22
Superhabit 3 – The Power of Planning and To-Do Lists	30
Superhabit 4 – The Power of Setting Goals	36
Superhabit 5 – The Power of Practice Questions	42
Superhabit 6 – The Power of Sleep	50
Superhabit 7 – The Power of Spaced Practice	58
Superhabit 8 – The Power of a Deliberate Mindset	66
Habits in Practice – The Pomodoro Technique	74
Habits in Practice – Flashcards	82
Habits in Practice – Using Mind Maps to Summarise and Recall	90
Habits in Practice – A Little Planning and Using Lists	98
Habits in Practice – Building Study Skills Like a Muscle	108
References	116

Introduction
Life Is Too Good for Bad Study

"Keep smiling,
because life is a beautiful thing
and there's so much to smile about."
– Marilyn Monroe,
American actress (1926–42)

SCOTT FRANCIS

FOUNDATION STUDY SKILLS FOR HIGH SCHOOL STUDENTS

Unlocking the 8 Superhabits of Study

Copyright © Scott Francis 2023

All rights reserved. No part of this book may be reproduced or transmitted in any form or by any means, electronic or mechanical, including photocopying, recording or by any information storage and retrieval system, without prior permission in writing from the publisher.

Published in 2023

Published by Amba Press
Melbourne, Australia
www.ambapress.com.au

Cover designer – Tess McCabe
Editor – Beth Browne

ISBN: 9781922607560 (pbk)
ISBN: 9781922607577 (ebk)

A catalogue record for this book is available from the National Library of Australia.

Introduction

As readers of this book, you will all be in different situations. Some of you will already have challenging academic goals and be driven to achieve at a high level academically. Let's refer to students who feel this way as academically ambitious students.

Others of you will be content passing subjects. There is nothing wrong with this ambition. Let's refer to students who feel this way as focused-on-passing students.

Over time your goals might change, and you might move from one group to the other. I know for me there have been times when I have been academically ambitious with my study and other times where I have been happy to just pass the study.

The point of defining academically ambitious students and focused-on-passing students is to see if we can find common ground between these two groups. I think it is possible, particularly around the idea of efficiency.

Whether you are academically ambitious or focused on passing, the common ground is that you almost certainly want to get the most out of your study time. No-one goes home with 10 maths questions for homework that should take 15 minutes to do and thinks, *How can I turn this 15 minutes of homework into 45 minutes?*

This is the core of this book.

I want to suggest some study habits and ideas that, whether you are academically ambitious or focused on passing, you will be able to use to gauge whether they might make you more efficient as a student.

One of the things in the world that makes me sad is bad study. Bad study looks like students struggling to get started, students trying to study while on their phone or social media, students trying to work for long periods of time without much progress, students who mucked around in class trying to do homework based on the classwork without the understanding to get started, and students who try to study in an environment full of distractions and take 90 minutes to do 30 minutes worth of study.

This makes me sad because for the student involved (and I hope this is not you – or soon won't be you) this is frustrating, time-wasting and stressful. You are battling yourself to get your study done, and you will not enjoy it.

There are too many good things in life – family, friends, sports, music, hobbies, entertainment, movies, being in nature – to spend it doing bad study.

If I could nudge you toward one thought with this short book it would be that life is too short for bad study.

When you are finding yourself doing bad study – and by 'bad study' I mean ineffective and distracted study – take a break, try another strategy or talk to some adults about what is happening. By reading this book you will build some habits that will move you away from bad study.

Which will be important because life is too good for bad study.

Why Superhabits?

When I started writing this book, I wanted to think about everything I knew about study and try to find a way of emphasising the most important elements.

I found 8 elements that I wanted to emphasise and called them the 8 Superpowers of Study.

Reflecting on this, I decided I didn't like this name. Superpowers sound like they could be magically bestowed on us, like the ability to jump buildings in a single bound.

That is when I moved to the idea of superhabits – the 8 Superhabits of Study. These are elements you can use to build better study habits; however, the responsibility lies with you to learn about, trial and use the habits. These habits are not superpowers. They are not going to magically become part of your practice. Instead, they are going to require effort on your part. It is not easy taking on a new habit. However, if you want to get more out of your study time, become more efficient as a student and have more time for the other great things in life, you might choose to work toward building these superhabits into your routines.

Keep an Eye on Effort, Not Just Time

As a teacher for over 12 years now, I often hear students talk about their study in terms of how many hours they put in, such as 'Over the weekend I spent 4 hours working on my science assignment'.

Time is not the only input into effective study. The intensity of the effort you put in will be important as well.

The intensity of your effort can be considered with questions such as:

- Did I work without distractions?
- Did I have a clear aim in mind when I started my study?
- Had I worked well in class to give me the best chance of effective study?
- Did I start early on my assignment or exam revision?
- Did I stay on task while studying?
- Did I take breaks, perhaps for a snack or exercise, so I was alert while studying?
- Did I leave my phone in the next room while I studied?

When you are thinking about study, try to think of it as a maths formula:

Study impact = Intensity of effort × Time

Most students focus on time as the key input into study. See if you can focus on the intensity of your effort as well and get more study impact from the same amount of time. After all, life is too good for bad study!

Introducing the 8 Superhabits of Study

A number of years ago I set myself a challenge – could I put the most important elements of study into a diagram that was simpler than the long presentations students often had to sit through about study skills.

The following diagram does that.

It has the 8 best habits I think a student who wants to be efficient with their time – and we all should want to be efficient with our time – should develop.

The diagram also tries to remind us of three other things:

1. A favourite saying of mine, that 'Life is too Good for Bad Study' – if you are making the commitment to study, do it well!
2. A reminder that study is not just about the time you put it, it is also about the effort you put into your study time. In fact, I think your study impact will be a mix of the time you put in, and the effort and focus while you work. I think of if as a maths formula: 'Study Impact = Intensity of Effort x Time'.
3. Study is about growing positive impact over time. I think of the analogy of a tree, that grows over time. Taking on a positive study habit will help water the 'tree' that represents growth as a learner.

We will learn more about the 8 habits, or superhabits as I call them, in this book. The diagram from the challenge I set myself to represent my most important ideas about study is opposite.

Superhabit 1
The Power of an A+ Effort in Class

"You can practise shooting eight hours a day, but if your technique is wrong, then all you become is very good at shooting the wrong way. Get the fundamentals down and the level of everything you do will rise."

– Michael Jordan, former NBA basketballer

The Basics

There is a reason I have chosen this as the first habit in this book: I think it is the most important. If you do a great job in class, it creates a foundation for you to build on. If you do a poor job in class, it leaves you with more work to do and the frustration of not having a good foundation in place to work from.

Let's face it, when you are sitting in class, you are surrounded by more resources than you will be at any other time in your study journey – a combination of teachers, peers, textbooks, classroom resources and computers.

Perhaps equally as important as the available resources is the concept of 'opportunity cost'. This is a challenging concept – one you might come across in Year 12 economics – but I think it illustrates an important point, so try to stick with it.

Opportunity cost considers what you give up by being in a situation. For example, once you choose to be at school, there is not a lot else that you could be doing at that time. Short of skipping school, there is no TV to watch, you can't be down at the movies and there is no chance of popping down to the beach for a swim.

Compare that to planning to study on a weekend. Instead of studying, there are a lot of options for you, from being out fishing to listening to music and from going to a movie to shopping with friends.

Given that the classroom is a low-opportunity-cost and resource-rich environment, where the basics of content are introduced, it should be the foundation of your study efforts.

How Does This Help with the 'How Do I Study?' Question?

An A+ effort in class is about building a great foundation for your study. And while it sounds easy to do, it is much harder in practice.

Here is an under-discussed secret that most students (and teachers) know: it is easy to look like you are working hard in class (later in the chapter I am going to call this 'academic compliance'). Conversely, it is hard to consistently work and learn effectively (I am going to call this 'academic intensity'). To see how well you are using class time, you might like to use the following statements to evaluate the quality of your classroom work:

- I don't just sit with friends in class, I sit with people who make me better as a learner.
- When I copy down notes, I make sure that I rewrite them in my own words and clarify anything I don't understand.

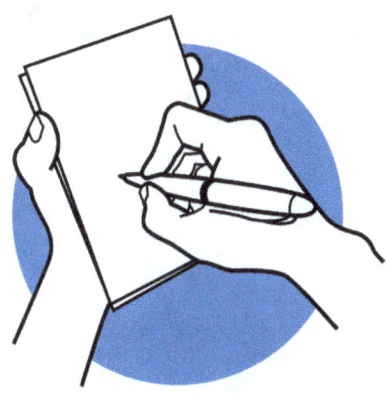

- When I get homework or an in-class task, my focus is not to complete it, but to complete the task at a high standard.
- When there is a short break in class – for example, the teacher has gone outside to talk with someone – I will find something useful to do during that time, such as reading ahead in the textbook.

- If the teacher leaves the classroom for a longer period of time, I will largely remain on task with my work.
- Regardless of whether I like the teacher or not, I work with them positively to get the most out of class time.

If you start answering 'yes' more often to these questions, you are increasingly building a great foundation for your study using class time.

Where Do We See this Habit in Other Environments?

In the world of elite sports, former NBA basketballer Michael Jordan remains among the most successful of them all. His quote at the start of this chapter reminds us of the link between practice and performance (performance in study being about creating assignments and completing exams). It is not unreasonable to think that the classroom is the 'practice venue' of learning – where we learn the fundamentals, practise new skills and get feedback, and push ourselves with our learning. If we aren't getting the most out of our practice time, we aren't building a base for the level of our academic performance to rise.

Any Boring Research to Support This?

I am going to cheat a little in this section, and instead of using other people's research, I am going to use a table that I have put together. It compares what I commonly see in class, which we might call 'academic compliance', with 'academic intensity'.

Academic compliance is about doing an acceptable job in class and meeting standards. In reality this is where most people sit – and that is OK if they want OK results. They will probably get on OK with teachers, parents and carers on the back of their academic compliance.

Academic intensity is the A+ effort during class and is far less common. Academic intensity is about getting the most out of class time.

Academic compliance is easy and common – and OK.

Academic intensity is challenging and rare.

Behaviours of Academic Compliance	Behaviours of Academic Intensity (An A+ Effort)
Not disruptive to the class	Interested in class – asking questions
Resources are available	Resources are available
Engaged enough to be moving through task sets	Completing tasks to a high standard
Quiety off task if unsupervised	Remains on task even when there is no supervision
Complete set homework to an acceptable standard	Homework completed early, with some extra work and attention to detail (eg attend turtoring for guidance on challenges)
Assignment/exam study started no more than 48 hours before the deadlines	Developing habits that see task started early
Sit with friends	Sit with people who have a positive impact on learning
Occasionally does work from other subjects in class	Focussed on the subject at hand
Writes down notes verbatim (word for word)	While writing notes, ensures that their notes make sense and is prepared to re-organise/re-phrase them

A Final Word

There aren't any other places that you can legitimately be during class time, so it makes sense to be working hard during this time. As the most resource rich learning environment – with peers, teachers, textbooks and laptops available – it should be the foundation of your study efforts. And don't kid yourself – while being academically compliant (looking like you are working hard) might be OK, it is academic intensity (actually working hard) that will get you ahead.

Your classroom effort largely dictates where you start the rest of your study efforts. An A+ effort in class gives you the advantage of starting ahead.

Superhabit 2
The Power of Single-Tasking

"You can't do big things if you are distracted by small things."

– Unknown

The Basics

Distractions are the enemy of effective study.

Perhaps the term 'single-tasking' is not familiar to you, so let's start by building an understanding of the concept. Single-tasking is the opposite of multi-tasking. Multi-tasking is the situation where we try to do several tasks at once – perhaps we are trying to do a little study with a YouTube video on, our mobile phone next to us and our email open as well.

The reality is that multi-tasking significantly reduces our capacity.

Single-tasking is different from multi-tasking. When we single-task we are focused on one thing and work to get rid of distractions.

If we can single-task while we are studying, staying focused and without distractions while we work, we will be more effective. We will be better at recalling more information later, completing tasks more quickly and being able to cope with complex tasks – all while experiencing less stress.

How Does This Help with the 'How Do I Study?' Question?

Let's not beat around the bush here, the biggest distractions we have while we are studying are 'virtual' – distractions from social media (unless you went all in on a MySpace account), email, messages, YouTube, app notifications and so on.

A focus on single-tasking means study without your phone out, without any other electronic distractions, in a quiet space and with no background distractions like TV or music with lyrics.

At my current school, I run afternoon study sessions for about three hours after school. At the end of each session I ask students, 'Are you happy with the work you got through?'. They almost always say yes, and they agree that a significant part of this is that they are studying without distractions, in a quiet classroom and with their phones away.

An idea that might help you single-task is the pomodoro technique, which we'll cover in more detail later in the book. With the pomodoro technique you study for a relatively short period of time – say, 20 to 30 minutes – without distractions. You then have a 5-minute break where you might catch up with some friends online, go for a walk or have a healthy snack, and then you get back to work. The benefit of this strategy is that you set yourself up in a low-distraction environment for a more manageable 20 or 30 minutes rather than trying the much more significant challenge of working for two hours without distractions.

So, to answer the 'How do I study?' question, if you can set yourself up in a low-distraction environment, with your phone on flight mode – or, even better, in the next room – and with the TV and other distractions out of the way, you will be in a great position for effective study.

Where Do We See this Habit in Other Environments?

In 2021, Chris Anstey, former NBA basketballer, professional basketball coach and Olympian, gave a presentation to a group of students I was working with about study and high performance. He talked about the rule he had with the professional basketball teams he coached: 'When we are improving ourselves, we put away our phones'. Getting rid of distractions was an important element in quality sports practice, just as it is with study.

Any Boring Research to Support This?

Larry Rosen is a Professor from California State University and author of the book The Distracted Mind. He summarised some of the key research around distractions in an article titled 'The Distracted Student Mind' (2017).

In the article, Rosen provided some statistics from research into the cost of distraction on study, which included the following:

- In a study watching actual students study, they struggled to work for even 15 minutes at a time before being distracted and spent 5 minutes out of a typical 15-minute study block distracted.
- Students who fail to single-task when they study report greater feelings of stress and take longer to complete their work.
- 75% of student distractions are from technology (phone, tablet or computer).

- Students who had the habit of immediately responding to messages tended to have lower grades.
- Multi-tasking reduces students' ability to remember what they are studying.

A Final Word

I want to finish with an emphasis on the research into distraction. Being distracted as you study increases stress, causes you to take longer to do your work and reduces your ability to remember what you are studying.

If you can build the habit of single-tasking into your study, you can expect to become more efficient at study.

Superhabit 3
The Power of Planning and To-Do Lists

"There are dreamers and there are planners. The planners make their dreams come true."

– Edwin Louis Cole,
American author (1922–2002)

The Basics

Having a plan is a stepping stone to getting work done. In this chapter, two planning tools are introduced: a weekly planner and a to-do list. I say they are introduced here because we are going to come back and look at the practical use of these tools later in the book.

The tools are pretty much exactly as they are named:

- A weekly planner is a tool that sets out your time over a week, where you can set aside some time for study (and all your other activities, including those you enjoy!).
- A to-do list is where you keep a record of the tasks you are working on, perhaps even broken down into smaller sections (for example, for an assignment you might break it down into research, writing a draft, seeking feedback and writing a final copy).

How Does This Help with the 'How Do I Study?' Question?

These two tools become a great foundation of planning.

Having a weekly planner allows you to have a plan for your time over the week and all your commitments – maybe a part-time job, sports, music, volunteering and study. It is also worth setting aside time for things you enjoy – perhaps a regular catch-up with friends or time to watch a movie on a Saturday afternoon.

Using a to-do list allows you to see the steps you have to work through to prepare for an upcoming assignment or exam. Breaking up tasks into smaller steps – for example, splitting an assignment into researching, drafting, getting feedback and writing the final copy – makes each task more realistic. Listing the steps should give you a clear idea of what you need to do an a little hint of pleasure every time you get to tick a step off the list as complete.

Neither are complex tools; however, together they allow you to see that you have some time strategically set aside for your study, and they are a way of breaking up tasks into manageably sized pieces that you can enjoy ticking off your to-do list.

Where Do We See this Habit in Other Environments?

Richard Branson (2017) wrote a blog on the habit of using to-do lists. As a successful businessperson, he talked about the benefits of making lists. Here are some of his thoughts from his own blog:

> *To say that life as an entrepreneur and business leader is busy is an understatement. So, in order to make sure I achieve everything that not only needs to get done but also everything I want to get done, I make lists – lots of them.*
>
> *I have always lived my life by making lists.*
>
> *Each day I work through these lists. By ticking off each task, my ideas take shape and plans move forward.*

If the habit of making lists is good enough to get the plans of one of the most successful businesspeople moving forward, then it is likely to be a useful tool to get your work as a student moving forward as well.

Any Boring Research to Support This?

There are two research focuses that I think are worth being aware of. The first can be found in an article written by Louise Chunn (2017) titled 'The Psychology of the To-Do List – Why Your Brain Loves Ordered Tasks'. Chunn's article gives three reasons why a to-do-list might help us:

1. They dampen anxiety about chaos.
2. They give us a structure.
3. They are proof that we have completed things (as we tick items off our list).

This is a great endorsement of the use of lists, but is there evidence that a weekly planner might help us as well? The same article looks at research by Masicampo and Baumeister (2011) that suggested people who had a plan toward a goal (for example, by writing down what they needed to do on a list and setting aside time in the future in a weekly planner) did not spend as much time thinking or worrying about what was coming up. Reducing the amount of worry that comes with school and study sounds like a worthwhile reason to spend a little time planning ahead!

A Final Word

It sounds simple. I wish I could make it sound more profound. However, I stand by the characterisation of having a weekly planner and using to-do lists as a superhabit. It provides a strong foundation for the when and what of your study, and that is a great starting point.

Superhabit 4
The Power of Setting Goals

"It is not enough to take steps which may someday lead to a goal; each step must be itself a goal and a step likewise."

— Johann Wolfgang von Goethe,
German author and scientist (1749–1832)

The Basics

Setting a goal, or even having an aim in mind, can help you be more deliberate with your study. This might be in the short term – for example, setting a goal for a study session. It might also be the long term – for example, setting a goal to improve a result in a subject over a semester.

There is a significant body of research that says that if you have a clear goal, both effort and performance are likely to be improved.

If there was one area to apply this idea of goals to your study, I would encourage it to be around your study sessions. If you have a clear goal in mind every time you sit down to study, you are likely to get more work done and feel better about ticking your goal off as complete at the end of your study session.

Examples of goals you might set in a study session are:

- Finish the maths problems started in class.
- Create a mind map of characters from the English novel being explored in class.
- Read a chapter of the English novel.
- Complete the bibliography for my history assignment.
- Create 15 flashcard questions from the science chapter.

These sorts of goals provide you with a clear focus on what you need to do as well as the chance to tick off the task at the end of the session and celebrate your progress.

How Does This Help with the 'How Do I Study?' Question?

Perhaps you have heard of students setting a goal for a term or over a semester. This is a reasonable idea, and something you might choose to do. However, I think initially the more useful way of using goals while you study is to have a clear goal in mind for each study session that you do.

For example, you might be sitting down to do some maths study. It makes sense to have a clear goal in mind for your study. Perhaps the goal might be to practise questions from two chapters of the textbook over the next 20 minutes.

You have a clear goal in mind, which gives you a clear direction for the next 20 minutes. At the end of that time (hopefully) you can tick off the goal as completed.

If you make the effort to have a clear goal in mind every time you sit down to study, it will help give your study session some focus – an important element in the 'How do I study?' question.

You might also choose to use a written goal to set a plan over a semester. For example, your goal might be to improve your maths grade over semester 2. You might then add some steps you want to take to be successful – for example, attend tutoring, sit closer to the front of class, do your homework regularly and start early when you have a maths assignment. With a written goal, and a plan, you put yourself in a strong position to be successful.

Where Do We See this Habit in Other Environments?

Bruce Lee was a high-achieving actor. Before his career as an actor, he wrote down a key goal for himself – now framed at Planet Hollywood – which drove his success. It was:

> My Definite Chief Aim
>
> I, Bruce Lee, will be the first highest paid Oriental superstar in the United States. In return I will give the most exciting performances and give the best of quality in the capacity of an actor. Starting 1970 I will achieve world fame and from then onward till the end of 1980 I will have in my possession $10,000,000. I will live the way I please and achieve inner harmony and happiness.

While Lee passed away before 1980, he was enormously successful – driven by a clear written goal.

Any Boring Research to Support This?

The key researcher into whether goals are effective is Edwin Locke, a psychologist and retired professor from the University of Maryland. In a summary of the body of research on setting goals (2002), he said that 'setting goals has been shown to increase performance on well over 100 different tasks'.

In other research, Angela Duckworth (2013), focused on the positive impact of setting goals for students and found that goals helped support better results for students.

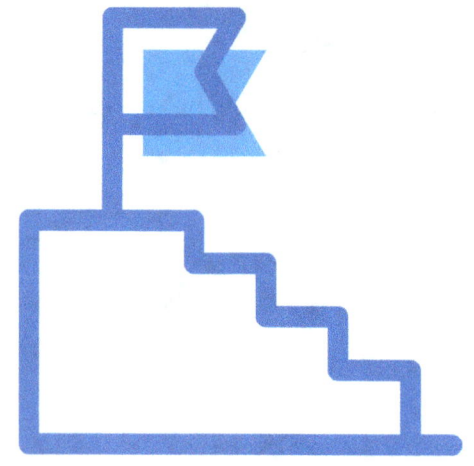

A Final Word

Sitting down to study is a great first step.

Sitting down to study with a clear goal in mind is even better.

If you can build the habit of having a clear goal in mind when you sit down for a study session, it will be a useful step in being an effective student.

Superhabit 5
The Power of Practice Questions

"Learn from yesterday, live for today, hope for tomorrow. The important thing is not to stop questioning."

– Albert Einstein,
theoretical physicist (1879–1955)

The Basics

We study best when we are actively involved with our work, and the best way of being actively involved is to be answering questions about what we are doing. These could be revision questions from the teacher, past exam paper questions, end-of-chapter questions, self-prepared questions (such as flashcards with a question on one side and an answer on the other) or questions the teacher asks in class. If the teacher asks someone else a question, prepare your own answer in your head and see how accurate it is.

I have a teaching colleague, Mr Flynn, who has an interesting take on the way many students study. He says most students study in a way that is similar to going to the gym and expecting to get fit by watching other people exercising. What he means is that many students study in a very passive, rather than active, way by doing things like:

- rereading the textbook
- highlighting
- re-reading notes.

Just like watching people exercise at the gym won't get you fit, rereading and highlighting are not effective ways to study, although they are the strategies many people use for their study.

The pinnacle of active study strategies is the use of practice questions. When you are finding questions to answer, you are forcing yourself to retrieve knowledge from your memory – a great way of checking what you know and deepening that knowledge by retrieving it from your memory.

How Does This Help with the 'How Do I Study?' Question?

Practice questions.

Practice questions.

Practice questions.

The simplest way to jump into active study is to practise answering questions during your study time.

When you answer a question from your memory – that is, without referring to your textbook, notes or the class PowerPoint – you are retrieving the information from your memory. The fancy name for this is 'retrieval practice'. This act of retrieval forces us to locate information from our memory, something that supports learning.

Retrieval practice is different from doing a multi-choice quiz. If there is a question with four possible answers, we are not actually retrieving the information from our memory, just recognising the correct information. This is useful, but not as useful as testing ourselves by retrieving the information from our memory.

Practice questions provide you with some crucial study information. They let you know what you know well and can retrieve from your memory. They also let you know what you need more practice with to be able to retrieve it from memory.

So where might you find yourself some practice questions? There are usually various sources of questions, including textbook questions, end-of-chapter questions, revision questions prepared by a teacher and previous tests. Peers from your class may also be able to provide practice questions – even siblings or adults at home might be able to help!

Even better than relying on another source for practice questions is to prepare some yourself. This can be done using flashcards. Write a question on one side of a flashcard and the answer on the other. You could prepare questions every two or three weeks during a unit of work and use them to test yourself. Writing the questions is a great study habit in itself, because it makes you reflect on what is the most important content that you have covered.

Another active study technique, very similar to using practice questions, is the idea of a mind-map test. To do this, give yourself a set period of time – say, 10 minutes – to write down everything you can recall about a topic. Start with the topic in the middle, then list the key headings down to the more important detail. It's like a practice question, but it requires you to recall all of the key work at the one time. Once you have finished, you can check back and see what you know well and what needs further learning.

If in your practice questions or mind-map test you find something that you don't know, you can take an active approach to learning the missing information. Write up a summary of what you need to get better with knowing, rewrite it a couple of times and then challenge yourself with some practice questions that force you to retrieve the information to see if you have made progress.

You could also swap flashcards with another classmate and see how you go with each other's practice questions!

Where Do We See this Habit in Other Environments?

Marcus Luttrell is a retired US Navy SEAL and recipient of the Purple Heart, a prestigious US military honour.

He reminds us that practice, which is what study is, is an important environment in which to get ready for the challenges of performance: 'You play like your practice, and practice how you play'.

In an exam, you are going to be answering questions from your memory. The best way to prepare for that challenge is to test your memory of the topic you are studying using practice questions.

Any Boring Research to Support This?

The short answer is there is a significant body of research that supports using practice questions as an effective and active study technique.

A great summary of this research is found in some work by Professor John Dunlosky and colleagues (2013), from Kent State University and published in Psychological Science in the Public Interest. They found that using practice questions as you study is:

- useful across a range of formats and topics
- easy to do
- relatively quick
- effective – it improves your grade without spending any extra time studying.

A Final Word

When you study, challenge yourself to be active with your study. The number 1 strategy to achieve this is to answer practice questions as often as you can. It is simple and effective, making it a powerful study strategy.

Superhabit 6
The Power of Sleep

"Sleep is an investment in the energy you need to be effective tomorrow."

– Tim Roth, English actor

The Basics

Sleep helps you function better as a person and as a learner.

As a teenager, 8 to 10 hours of sleep per night will support the key elements of learning, including memory, problem-solving ability and a positive mood, and it will help with your ability to concentrate on learning the next day.

If I had to emphasise just one of these benefits, it would be the role that sleep plays in helping transfer your learning from today into your longer-term memory. When you are at school, and studying, you are hoping that knowledge and skills will sit in your memory so you can use them later. Researchers Jensen and Snider (2013) emphasised that 'adequate sleep plays a critical role in memory consolidation'.

There are a couple of challenges with sleep that you should be aware of. The first of these is the impacts of caffeine. Caffeine can take a long time to be processed by the body, with some experts suggesting caffeinated drinks consumed from midafternoon (2 pm) can negatively impact on sleep. Caffeine might come from coffee, iced coffee, cola drinks or energy drinks – although there is a strong argument that you are better off avoiding energy drinks altogether.

The second challenge to quality sleep is the blue light emitted from screens. This blue light from screens (including computers, phones and tablets) can delay the onset of sleep, so working on a screen late into the night can, rather unhelpfully, further reduce your ability to sleep.

How Does This Help with the 'How Do I Study?' Question?

If someone gave me the challenge of taking a straight-A student and turning them into a C student by doing just one thing, the one thing I would do is stop that student from getting enough sleep. I would have them up late at night (indeed until early in the morning) playing computer games, drinking energy drinks and using social media. There would be a series of negative impacts for the student in question. They would not remember their study as well (sleep helps in memory formation), their ability to work in class the next day would be reduced, and they would feel higher levels of stress.

What is the point of me thinking about this rather mean challenge? It helps highlight how important sleep is for learning. If you can get 8 to 10 hours of quality sleep every night, you will build a foundation that allows your brain to work well and your learning will be more effective.

VicHealth, in a report entitled Sleep and Mental Wellbeing (2017), suggested that teenagers are getting 6.5 to 7.5 hours of sleep per night, rather than the suggested 8 to 10 hours per night.

A focus on getting enough sleep is the key here. Michael Nagel, a professor at the University of the Sunshine Coast and learning expert, talks about regulating sleep in a positive way, including:

- keeping technology out of the bedroom
- stopping using devices/laptops in the evening, maybe around 9 pm
- eating well and exercising
- considering reading a book, meditating or deep breathing if falling asleep is hard.

Importantly, if you are having trouble finding a routine that allows you to get the 8 to 10 hours a night that you need and you have tried the suggestions above, have a conversation with a trusted adult (such as an adult at home, a GP, a teacher or a school counsellor) and start looking for a solution.

Where Do We See this Habit in Other Environments?

LeBron James is among the greatest basketballers of all time. He is adamant that one area he focuses on to be able to perform at his best is getting enough sleep. Speaking on a Tim Ferriss podcast he said:

> *Sleep's the best way for your body to physically and emotionally be able to recover and get back to 100% as soon as possible. Now, will you wake up and feel 100%? There are some days you don't. So some days you feel better than others. But the more, and more, and more time that you get those eight – if you can get nine hours of sleep, that's amazing.*

Any Boring Research to Support This?

For this research, let's go to the source of one of the great universities of the world, Harvard in the United States, and a direct quote from an article titled 'Sleep, Learning, and Memory' (Harvard University, 2007, p. 8):

> *In the view of many researchers, evidence suggests that various sleep stages are involved in the consolidation of different types of memories and that being sleep-deprived reduces one's ability to learn ... the overall evidence suggests that adequate sleep each day is very important for learning and memory.*

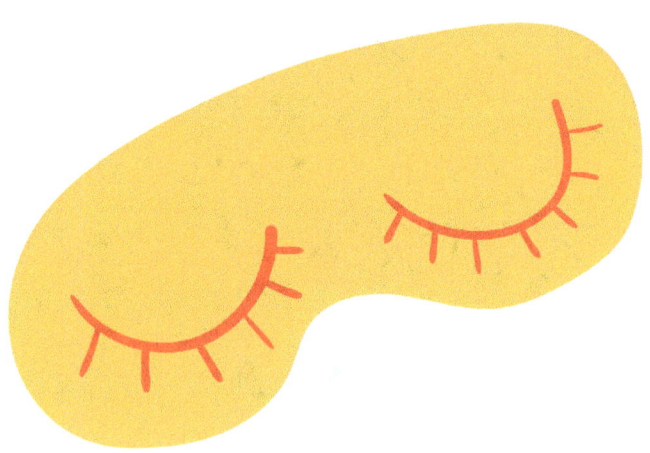

A Final Word

Most people know that they feel happier and healthier after quality sleep. If you are an ambitious student looking to get the most out of your learning, 8 to 10 hours of quality sleep each night is going to support you on that journey by helping you recall what you have been studying, helping you solve problems and assisting you to be ready to learn again the next day.

Superhabit 7
The Power of Spaced Practice

"The secret to getting ahead is getting started."

– Mark Twain,
American writer (1835–1910)

A Few Words ...

Before we jump into this chapter, I want to explain what spaced practice is. Spaced practice refers to having small amounts of practice spread over time. For example, a typical high school student might learn something in week 1 of term and then do some revision the night before their exam in week 9 of term. In this way they have two points of practice before the exam: when they learned the content and when they did some revision the night before the exam.

Compare that to another high school student who, in week 4 of term also sits down to write some practice questions about what they learned in the first four weeks of term. They then test themselves using the practice questions in week 6 of term. In week 8, when their teacher gives them a revision sheet, they do the questions that night. This second student has more practice opportunities over the term, spaced over time, and research suggests they will get a better result even if both students have spent the same amount of time studying (the first student might have spent more time cramming the night before the exam, for example).

The Basics

Spaced practice is the act of revisiting material between when it is learned and when it is tested. By revising two or three times between learning and testing, the recall of information is significantly improved.

In effect, this is the opposite of cramming. Rather than leaving all the revision until a day or two before the exam, spaced practice encourages us to do some revision well before the exam to increase our recall during the exam.

I am so enthusiastic about the possible impact of this habit that I don't want to wait until later in this chapter to share some research published by Carpenter, Cepeda, Rohrer, Kang and Pashler (2012), who looked at how well high school students remembered history facts. They split a group of students into two. Both had the same amount of time revising content; however, one group used spaced practice, doing their revision between when they learned the information and when they were tested. The spaced practice group had results 50% higher than the other group, even though they spent no extra time studying.

How Does This Help with the 'How Do I Study?' Question?

Let's be honest, most of us rely on cramming to get us through when we are studying. The night before an exam is an important time to be studying; however, going beyond this last-minute study and getting in some early revision can improve your results and decrease stress levels.

The bottom line: if you can add some study activities well before the exam, they are going to improve your results.

Let's put a clear timeframe around spaced practice and say that it is revision activities that happen more than three days before an exam.

In practice this might mean simple activities like:

- building a flowchart of an important topic well before the exam, so that you have a visual summary as a study resource

- creating and using flashcards with questions and answers, which you create as a topic is taught, aiming to have most of these prepared more than three days before an exam

- completing end-of-chapter revision questions or revision questions from class – a great example here might be a revision sheet given to you by a teacher a week before an exam (completing the revision sheet as soon as possible is a great spaced practice activity)

- setting aside some time to work on study tasks (creating a flowchart/flashcards or completing revision questions) before the final week leading up to the exam.

Where Do We See this Habit in Other Environments?

The NBA is an interesting high-performance environment. During the season, players play 3–4 games per week, plus travel. There is not a huge amount of time to work on their individual games. That makes the off-season particularly important.

Giannis Antetokounmpo is one of the best players in the NBA, playing for the Milwaukee Bucks. As great a player as he is, he is a poor free-throw shooter. A good free-throw shooter might make 80% of their free-throws; he makes around 70%. This becomes the focus of his improvement during his off-season. It wouldn't make sense to base his improvement around two big practice sessions – one at the start of the off-season and one at the end. Improvement comes through regular and focused practice, which is the core of what we have been talking about with spaced practice and study. Indeed, in his own words he talks about what he must do to improve:

> *It's simple. Just go back. Shoot more. Focus on your technique. Take it step by step. Just shoot more. That's it. The more you shoot, the more you work on it, the better you get. There's no secret in that.*

Any Boring Research to Support This?

Hermann Ebbinghaus was a researcher more than 100 years ago, yet his research still appears on the Queensland Curriculum and Assessment Authority website, talking about the importance of revising work regularly, or spaced practice.

The following graph illustrates the core of his work – the more frequently you revisit material, the more likely you are to be able to recall it in the future. (Where you see the word 'reviewed', think of a spaced practice strategy that might be used here, such as creating a flowchart, completing revision questions or creating flashcards with questions). This is the challenge for students: are you prepared to make that effort to revisit information between when it was first learned and the pre-exam cramming period, thus laying the foundation for improved results?

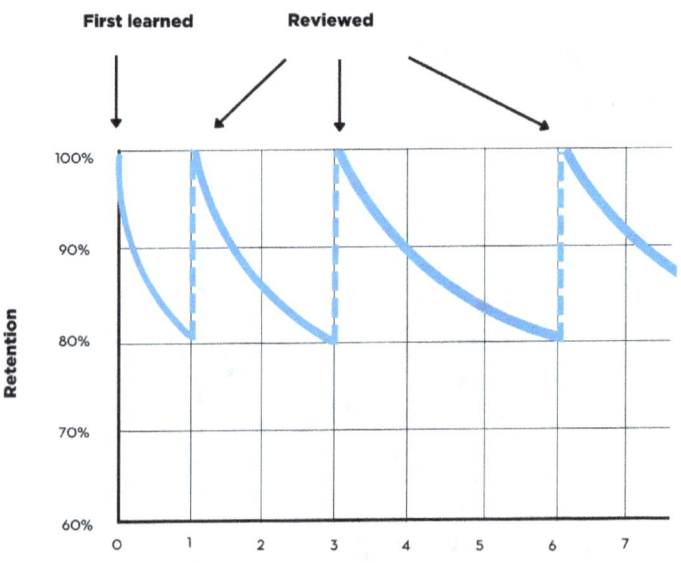

Typical Forgetting Curve for Newly Learned Information

A Final Word

There is no secret that the night or two before an exam is a busy time for revision. However, an investment of study time before the last week leading up to an exam pays dividends at exam time, allowing you to recall information more easily and to feel less stressed.

Superhabit 8
The Power of a Deliberate Mindset

"The greatest weapon against stress is our ability to choose one thought over another."

— William James,
American philosopher and psychologist
(1842–1910)

The Basics

An important part of our learning journey is that we have choices regarding how we think about our learning.

When I was young, I read a lot of Charlie Brown cartoons. I remember one that said the secret to happiness is to have a convertible (car) and a lake. When it is raining, you can be happy that the lake is filling up. When it is sunny, you can be happy that you can take your convertible for a drive. In some ways this is the core of the idea of mindset, the idea that you might be able to influence your attitudes to situations.

There are two ideas I would like to propose that might help you influence your mindset. They are:

1. I am here now; I might as well do my best.
2. Challenging work, and learning from mistakes, helps grow our ability.

How Does This Help with the 'How Do I Study?' Question?

The attitude that we take toward our study will influence the outcomes that we get.

The first attitude I want to suggest comes from a presentation I attended that was given by former NBA player and Olympic basketballer Chris Anstey.

Chris was a very good tennis player as a junior athlete. In Year 11 he was asked to fill in for his brother's basketball team. He did not want to go but was finally convinced by his mum. On the way to play the game, he decided he would be deliberate about his thinking – his mindset. He decided that if he was going anyway, he might as well do his best. He got some instructions from the coach and tried his best. It turned out he was very effective – he scored 52 points and his team won. His playing ability was noticed by some senior basketball coaches, and this led to opportunities to improve his basketball until he was getting paid to play professionally in the NBA. His mindset – I might as well try my best – contributed to the opportunities he created. In the same way, this mindset can help with your study. You are there. Sitting down. With work to do. Why not give it your best effort?

The second idea is that of **growth mindset**. This is a mindset idea from Carol Dweck, a psychology professor at Stanford University. The core of this idea is that when confronted with work you find hard or mistakes you have made (for example, a poor result in an exam), it is a great time to learn and increase your capacity. There are many people who believe that they cannot get better at areas of their life – they might say, for example, 'I'm just not a maths person'. This is an example of a **fixed mindset**. Someone with a growth mindset will say, 'I'm not great at maths at the moment, but with work I will improve'. A growth mindset will also lead someone to think, *This work is hard, but if I stick with it, it will improve my capacity*. A growth mindset will also lead someone to say, 'I made some mistakes here, but if I can learn from these mistakes, it will improve my capacity'. A growth mindset leads to improvement.

Where Do We See this Habit in Other Environments?

Ash Barty is a superstar of Australian sport and winner of the Australian Open, the French Open and Wimbledon. While a large part of her success is in her tennis ability, she was also supported by Ben Crowe, her mindset coach.

If being deliberate about mindset can help someone at the highest levels of competitive sport, I think it can also be a useful tool for students.

Any Boring Research to Support This?

Carol Dweck is a researcher and psychologist from Stanford University. In her book *Mindset: The New Psychology of Success* (2006) Dweck gives specific examples of what a growth mindset – the mindset that supports improvement – looks like in a situation where you get a poor result in an early test in a subject. The growth mindset reactions to this include:

- *I need to try harder in class.*
- *I have to work harder, but I have the rest of the semester to improve my result.*
- *I'll think about studying harder for the next test.*
- *I'll look at what was wrong with my test and resolve to do better.*
- *I'll work harder on my next test and speak to the teacher to get some feedback.*

You might be able to see how a deliberate mindset helps people get the best out of situations that don't seem so positive at first (for example, poor test results). A focus on what behaviour can be adjusted to do better is a positive response to the disappointment of a poor test result.

A Final Word

If you can challenge yourself to be deliberate about your attitudes to your study, this can support your efforts as a student.

If your motto for study sessions becomes 'I am here now; I might as well do my best', that will help make your study time worthwhile.

If you can look at challenging work, mistakes and poor results as opportunities to increase your capacity – that is, if you choose to put a growth mindset into practice – it will help your improvement.

Habits in Practice
The Pomodoro Technique

"By prevailing over all obstacles and distractions, one may unfailingly arrive at their chosen goal or destination."
— Christopher Columbus,
Italian explorer (1451–1506)

What Is the Pomodoro Technique?

The pomodoro technique is an idea that has been around for a few decades. It came from someone who used a kitchen timer in the shape of a tomato (pomodoro is the Italian word for tomato) to time short study efforts, followed by quick breaks.

This led to the technique that focuses on using relatively short periods of time for study (say, 15 to 25 minutes) and then having a quick break before another study burst.

An overall study session might look like this:

- 20 minutes of study time
- 5-minute break to check the phone, message some friends, do a guided meditation or put on your favourite song
- 20 minutes of study time
- 15-minute break to have a snack and go for a quick walk – by the way, exercise makes an outstanding rest break as it promotes brain activity (great for learning) and increases alertness (also great for learning)
- 20 minutes of study time.

By the end of this session you will have 'banked' an hour of quality study, without ever having worked for more than 20 minutes at a time.

Habits in Practice

How Does This Help with the 'How Do I Study?' Question?

The pomodoro technique gives you a structure to use around your study. Not only that – it has a few little tricks that might help you get started on your study.

The first trick is around the shorter period of time for each pomodoro study effort. We already know that distractions (often mobile phones and social media) can hurt our study efforts. However, if we are sitting down for a long study effort – for example, an hour and a half of study – it is really hard to put our phone away for that long. In contrast, putting our phone away for 20 minutes is a more realistic goal.

The second trick comes from the momentum of getting started. It is much easier to sit down to do 20 minutes of work rather than try to get started on an hour and a half of work. This might be especially true after a long day at school. Twenty minutes of concentration and effort is doable, and easier to jump into, compared to an hour and a half. Once we get started with the 20 minutes of work, we have momentum on our side and can have a quick break before moving on to the next task.

The third trick is around having an objective in mind (a way of setting a goal for each session). When you are working for a 20-minute session it is easy to have a clear goal in mind (for example, completing some maths problems, finding some articles for a topic or creating a reference list), and that helps us to be efficient as students.

The fourth and final trick is one of celebration. Having a goal and completing it within the 20 minutes feels good and allows you to celebrate progress. In fact, Dr Ralph Ryback (2016) wrote an article published in Psychology Today where he described setting and completing a task in the following way:

> *The satisfaction of ticking off a small task is linked with a flood of dopamine (which makes you feel good). Each time your brain gets a whiff of this rewarding neurotransmitter, it will want you to repeat the associated behaviour.*

Which Superhabits Does the Pomodoro Technique Support?

The pomodoro technique works with two key superhabits, those of single-tasking and setting a goal.

It supports **single-tasking** because putting the mobile phone away for 2 hours is probably unrealistic, while setting up a distraction-free environment for 20 minutes of work is much more realistic.

It supports **setting a goal** because starting each 20-minute block with a clear goal in mind focuses your effort and gives you a positive feeling as you complete each task.

The pomodoro technique also allows us to work with our concentration span – at the best of times our concentration span might only be 15 to 25 minutes, or possibly a little less after a long day at school. Using shorter periods of study, separated by breaks, is kinder to our brain.

What Do I Need to Make This Work?

The recipe for the pomodoro technique is easy. You need a distraction-free space, 20 minutes of time to commit to your work, a timer (preferably not your mobile phone, which is best left in the next room) and a clear idea about the task you are working on.

A Final Word

The pomodoro technique – studying for short periods of time with regular breaks and a clear goal in mind for each study session – is a great way of organising your study. Work hard. Break hard. Get your work done!

Habits in Practice
Flashcards

"Repetition is the key to real learning."

– Jack Canfield,
American author and motivational speaker

What Are Flashcards?

Flashcards are a simple and effective study technique that allows you to create some practice questions and then use the questions to test yourself.

There are several sources of questions for your flashcards, including questions from your textbook, revision questions from your teacher and questions that you write yourself. Writing at least some of the questions yourself is a great study strategy in itself, as it encourages you to think about the most crucial information you have learned, and the style of questions you might find in your exam.

The flashcard itself is simple – a piece of paper or card that allows you to write a question on one side and an answer on the other. Officeworks sells index cards that are about 12 cm x 8 cm, which is ideal, and they are sold in a box of 500, so there is the potential for plenty of questions! However, there is nothing magic about flashcards written on card, and a piece of A4 paper cut into 4 pieces works just as well.

Let's use a simple example. I teach a lot of junior maths. Let's say a student is doing a unit on area, and in the first week they revise the rules for calculating the area of a shape. The student might put together the following flashcards, with the question on one side and the answer on the other.

Question Side of the Flashcard	Answer Side of the Flashcard
What is the area of a square with a side of 5 cm?	Rule: Area of square = side² = 5² = 25 cm²
What is the area of a triangle with a base of 7 cm and a perpendicular height of 10 cm?	Rule: Area of triangle = ½ base x perp. height = ½ x 7 x 10 = 35 cm²
What is the area of a circle with a circumference of 10 cm?	First: find the radius = circum. ÷ 2 = 10 ÷ 2 = 5 cm Rule: Area of circle = ϖr² = 78.6 cm²

How Does This Help with the 'How Do I Study?' Question?

Flashcards are a simple way of approaching your revision.

As you learn content over a term or semester, you can use that content to make some flashcards with questions and answers – like I demonstrated with the area questions for maths.

You can then use those flashcards to test yourself. As you try to answer each question, you can sort the flashcards into two piles, those that you answered correctly, and those that you struggled with.

Finally, you can take the flashcard questions that you struggled with and go back to your notes, textbook or teacher and find the correct answer.

Which Superhabits Do Flashcards Support?

1. **The habit of spaced practice:** You can use flashcards to regularly revise your content over the term, rather than leaving your study to the last minute.

2. **The habit of using practice questions:** Answering practice questions is a great way to study. Using flashcards is all about this!

3. **Retrieval:** While retrieval is not actually a superhabit, it is a valuable study technique that you utilise by making and using flashcards. Retrieval is about making yourself answer questions, and in doing so you are retrieving the information you are trying to learn from your memory. This is much better that just reading information – you are actually checking that you know the information and can use it to answer a question.

What Do I Need to Make This Work?

The bottom line is that you need very little to make this work – paper and scissors are all you need in practice.

Some organisation is also important, as you want to use the flashcards over the course of a term or semester, so find a safe space to store them. I have seen students have a second pencil case that they use for keeping their flashcards for a semester.

A Final Word

If I had to nominate one study technique that students in years 7 to 10 should use, it would be flashcards. They are a simple, proven and practical way to study.

Habits in Practice
Using Mind Maps

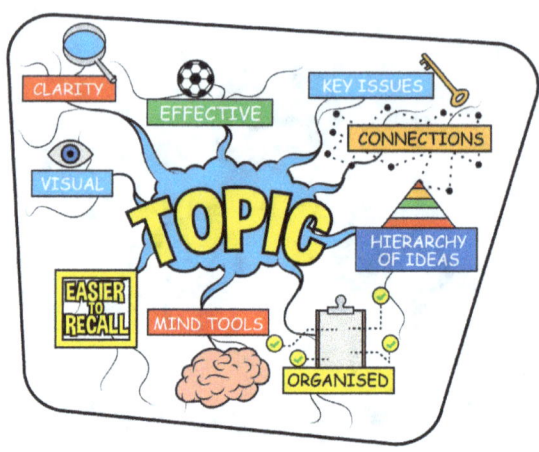

"A picture paints a thousand words."
— Unknown

What Is a Mind Map?

A mind map is a visual learning aid, as shown in the example below. It sets out the information about a topic, breaking it into key sub-topics and then the information that flows from that. I suspect that as students most of you will have come across mind maps as a method to organise data. This chapter builds on that idea to show how a mind map might be a useful study tool.

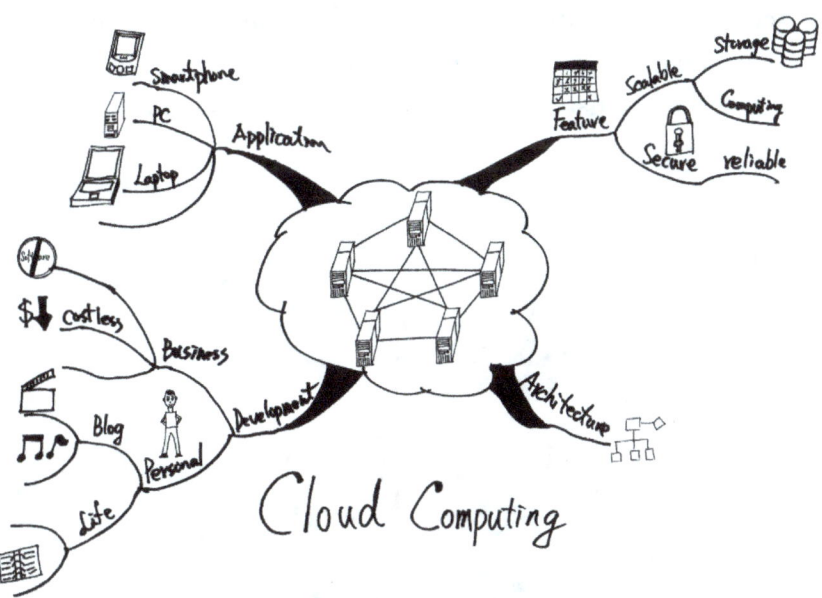

There are two study activities where a mind map might be useful:

- creating a summary of content
- testing what you know on a topic by creating a mind map from memory (maybe as a 10-minute challenge).

There are a variety of theories as to why mind maps work as a summary tool, including:

- the brain might recall a picture better than it does a block of text (remembering that a mind map is a picture)
- a mind map allows you to emphasise the key sub-topics (closer to the centre of the diagram) and links between ideas (you can draw lines between them)
- colour can be used for different topics, which helps to organise topics.

How Does This Help with the 'How Do I Study?' Question?

Mind maps fit into a category of learning tools called graphic organisers. They are acknowledged as an effective way to organise information for learning because you can see connections between material, you are organising the most important material as one image and you can see the most important topics toward the centre of most mind maps.

Mind maps support two specific study activities.

1. The first study activity is building a summary of a topic of work.
2. The second study activity is using a mind map as a way of testing exactly what you can recall about a topic.

If you use a mind map over the course of a topic of work, you can build a mind map related to the topic of work over time. For example, you might keep a piece of A3 paper in the back of your subject notebook, and every two weeks you add the recently learned information about the topic. Even if you don't organise your thoughts in a mind map regularly, it can be a strategy used toward the end of a topic to summarise what you have learned.

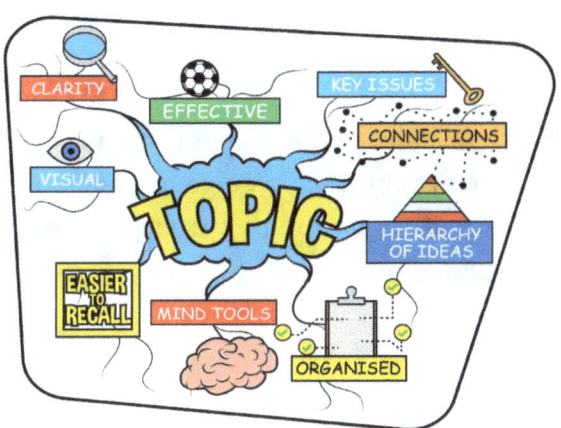

The second strategy is to use a mind map as a way of testing your ability to recall knowledge on a topic. To do this you start with a blank piece of paper and a time period in mind – say, 10 minutes. Your challenge is to write down everything you know about the topic in 10 minutes. For example, let's say you are studying a unit on maths, your challenge might be to write down as many of the maths rules that you have studied for the topic in 10 minutes.

The following image is an example of a mind map that has been used to put together the content from a maths topic related to geometry. You can see it presents what would normally be a number of smaller topics in the one mind map.

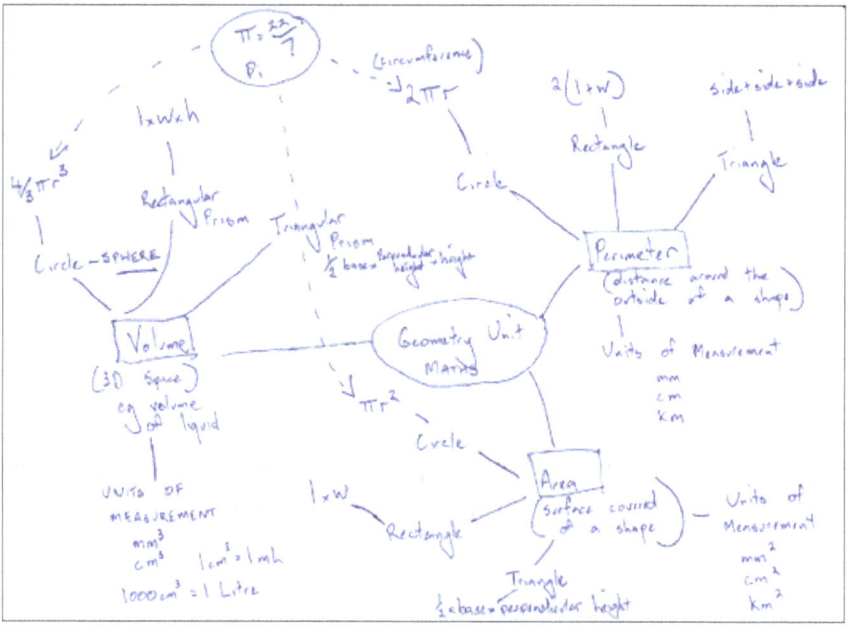

While we have not talked much about the application of mind maps to assignments, they can be a great way of organising your assignment information around the structure of your assignment – as a planning tool.

Which Superhabits Do Using Mind Maps Support?

If you are using mind maps to summarise information before a test, or while working on an assignment, that is a great example of the habit of **spaced practice** (starting early on tasks).

If you are using mind maps to test your knowledge, that is a great example of the habit of **using practice questions**. The question in this case is very broad – create a mind map that shows you everything that you know on a topic – but it does require you to retrieve information from your memory.

What Do I Need to Make This Work?

There is not a lot that is needed to make a mind map. A piece of A3 or A4 paper is a great start. Add to that a pen, a pencil or coloured pens/pencils, and you are ready to go. Colour can be useful to highlight information that fits together or information that is linked.

A Final Word

Mind maps are a simple study tool. They give you two useful strategies. The first is a way of summarising information as you learn about a topic. The second is to test yourself on what you know about a topic by creating a mind map from memory.

Habits in Practice
A Little Planning and Using Lists

"In planning for battle, I have always found that plans are useless, but planning is indispensable."

— Unknown

What Type of Planning or Lists Might a Student Use?

We looked at this topic as a superhabit earlier in the book and, because it is such a practical topic, we are looking at it again as an effective superhabit that can be put in practice.

We identified two planning documents that students should consider using. The first is a weekly planner, so there are definite study times (and blocks of fun) set aside in your week. The second is a to-do list, so that when tasks are mounting up, you use the list to set out what needs to be done, and you can tick off tasks as they are complete.

How Does This Help with the 'How Do I Study?' Question?

Here are two very specific suggestions to help get better organised with your study and, as we will see later, suggestions that might help you enjoy your study more and feel less stressed.

Let's start with the first idea: having a weekly study organiser. This is a way of setting out all your commitments over the course of a week. I have set out an example following this paragraph. In this example, the student:

- has a part-time job
- plays basketball
- sets aside some time to hang out with friends on Sunday
- identifies some tutoring opportunities at school that they might take advantage of
- sets out some study times for subjects
- schedules some time for assignment work on a Saturday morning.

	Monday	Tuesday	Wednesday	Thursday	Friday	Saturday	Sunday
Before school		Maths tutorial					
Lunch-time						10am–1pm local library	
3–4pm				English tutorial opportunity	Maths and English	Basketball game	Movies/shopping with friends
4–5pm		Maths and English	Basketball training	Humanities and electives	Work		
7–8pm	Humanities and electives		Humanities and electives		Work		
8–9pm					Work		

100 Foundation Study Skills

Before I get you to jump into making a weekly planner yourself, I want to highlight two points.

The first point is that it is a great idea to include some fun activities in your weekly plan. Let's face it, it is going to be tough to stick to a timetable that has no fun elements at all. Indeed, Douglas Barton (2016), in an article titled 'Three Things Top Performing Students Know That Their Peers Miss', identified that students who cram their weekly timetable full of study and nothing else are not able to commit to their schedule – after all, balance and fun are important too – and end up quickly giving up. On the other hand, students who add enjoyable activities tend to stick to their schedule much better.

The second point is that your weekly planner does not have to be followed precisely. If you find yourself well on top of your maths and English one night, find something else to do there. No assignment work at the moment? Do a little revision in that study session instead. A key point of this planning is that it allows you to feel that you are prepared. If you are starting to feel that you are falling behind in your maths, for example, you know that you have identified a definite time and the tutoring opportunity every week where you can catch up. It is almost like you have a plan even before you know you have a challenge.

The following is a blank weekly planner – you could jot down your own weekly plan in the space, remembering the benefits of including some enjoyable activities alongside your study. Of course, it will be equally easy to make one by hand or electronically.

	Monday	Tuesday	Wednesday	Thursday	Friday	Saturday	Sunday
Before school							
Lunch-time							
3–4pm							
4–5pm							
7–8pm							
8–9pm							

Let's move to the second habit – making a to-do list. Once again, there is nothing special here. It is just taking the time to set out all the tasks that need to be done, knowing that you have the time to do them (the beauty of the weekly plan), and then enjoying ticking them off as you complete each task.

There is research to support these study suggestions, which we looked at earlier in the book when we considered planning and to-do lists as a superhabit.

An article by Louise Chunn (2017) titled 'The Psychology of the To-Do List – Why Your Brain Loves Ordered Tasks' gives three reasons why a to-do list might help us:

1. They dampen anxiety about chaos.
2. They give us a structure.
3. They are proof that we have completed things (as we tick items off our list).

This is a great endorsement of the use of lists, but is there evidence that a weekly planner might help us as well? The same article looks at research by Masicampo and Baumeister (2011) that suggested people who had a plan toward a goal (for example, by writing down what they needed to do on a list and setting aside time in the future in a weekly planner) did not spend as much time thinking or worrying about what was coming up. That sounds like the ideal reason to spend a little time planning ahead!

Keep in mind the comment made earlier in the book about the pleasure we get ticking a task off a to-do list, another benefit of this strategy.

Which Superhabits Do the Use of a Weekly Planner and To-Do Lists Support?

As well as being a superhabit in itself, using a weekly planner and to-do lists supports a number of other superhabits.

Both a weekly plan and writing a to-do list support the habit of **setting goals**. The list can be seen as a series of smaller goals, which are ticked off as they are completed. A weekly planner helps you because it reserves time for you to work on your goals, whether that be ticking off items on your to-do list or working towards a larger goal you may have set – for example, improving in a subject.

Both the weekly planner and to-do lists support the idea of **mindset**. If you use these tools, you are choosing the mindset of someone with a level of planning and purpose to support their work. Research suggests ticking tasks off a to-do list makes us feel good and supports a mindset that says study can be both valuable and satisfying.

Finally, the habit of **spaced practice**, effectively starting your work early, is supported by having planned time in your weekly planner and a to-do list that identifies important tasks and allows you to get started on them earlier than if you were less organised.

What Do I Need to Make This Work?

The good news is that you can make your own to-do lists or weekly planner with 2 pieces of A4 paper and a pen.

There are electronic organisers that you might compare and see if one works for you.

For my own work, I like a laminated piece of paper with a permanent weekly schedule and a permanent to-do list printed on the paper. I then use a whiteboard marker to jot my plans in. I find this a great mix of permanent and flexible – permanent enough to pin up on a noticeboard and flexible enough to rub things out or add things in when needed.

A Final Word

Two simple organisational tools – a weekly planner and a to-do list – might help you feel a little less stressed and a little better about getting your work done and encourage you to get ahead with your study, making them well worth thinking about as possible study tools.

Habits in Practice
Building Study Skills Like a Muscle

"The brain is like a muscle. When it is in use we feel very good. Understanding is joyous."

– Carl Sagan,
scientist and author (1934–96)

The Final Chapter

Here we are, at the final chapter of this book. Thanks for reading this far!

I want to leave you with one final thought: perhaps if we think of the brain as a muscle, it might give us some useful insights into how to best study.

Let me explain why it might be useful to think of the brain as a muscle using 4 different ideas:

- the way prior learning impacts results
- the idea of a growth mindset
- the benefits of focused work
- the importance of active study (especially answering questions).

Let's look at these in turn.

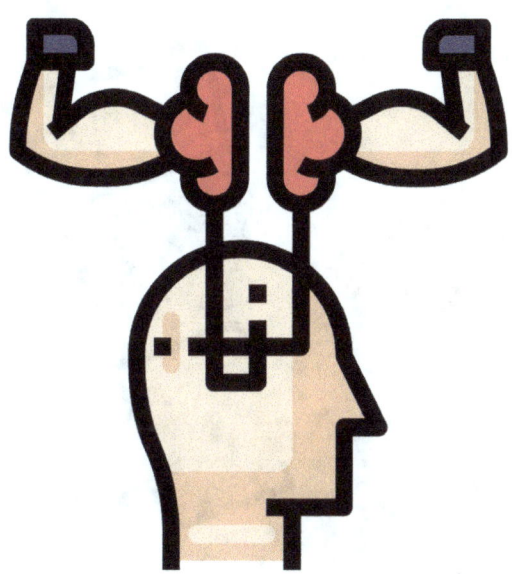

Prior Learning

Let's start with the way prior learning impacts results. Educational researcher John Hattie identified that out of all the elements that influence how well we learn, our prior knowledge is one of the most significant. That makes sense. Say I am doing a unit in Year 8 maths on probability. If I did well in Year 7 probability, I am likely to be in a strong position to do well again this year.

This suggests that as we work to improve as students, we should be patient and expect to see improvements over time. We are building our prior learning and a base for future study.

Just like I could not expect to go to the gym for the first time one month and then enter a bodybuilding contest the next, we should expect that it will take some time to build our capacity as we improve our study skills and efforts and build our base of prior learning.

Growth Mindset

We looked at the theory of the growth mindset earlier in the book. The one-sentence summary of the theory is that we grow our capacity when we stick with challenging work and don't give up, and when we make mistakes and learn from them.

This is a lot like the gym analogy. If I wander down to the gym every afternoon and do 4 sit-ups and then go home, I really can't expect to be much fitter, even if I keep going to the gym for a while. Just like muscles won't get stronger on a simple workout, neither will our brain. If I spend time doing the 2 times table (2 x 1 = 2; 2 x 2 = 4; 2 x 3 = 6 etc), I am not going to get smarter. Just like a muscle needs a challenge to grow, so does the brain. Persevering with challenging work, not giving up, and learning from mistakes – these are the acts that will grow the capacity of our brains.

I often think that a mistake today is like the push-up that we can't quite do. It shows us that we don't have the capacity to do it – yet. Sticking with the learning, just like we might stick with the routine of push-ups, will get us the improvement to get the question correct in the future.

The Benefits of Focused Work

I don't know how many of you will have come across the training concept of HIIT, which stands for high-intensity interval training. In this style of training, short bouts of intense exercise give good results.

Just as high-intensity workouts are great for the body, I think they are ideal for you as you study. The pomodoro technique we looked at in Chapter 9 is the brain equivalent of a HIIT session – get into the work, study with intensity and without distraction, and then have a break.

The Importance of Active Study

The example of the person who goes to the gym and does 4 sit-ups is relevant in this discussion. Going to the gym won't make that person fit, but the work they do while they are there will. And clearly it is going to have to be more than 4 sit-ups.

In the same way, sitting down to study won't get you results, but being active as a student while you study will. While there are times that reading, underlining and highlighting will be part of your study, the best results will be from the more active strategies, like creating a summary, and using the most active strategy of them all – answering practice questions without looking at your textbook, notes or class PowerPoint.

One Last Word

Finally, just like a person almost certainly won't be able to join a gym one week and then be lifting huge weights the next, it will take time to build the habits that support great study. Try to recognise the small pieces of improvement – the exam that was a little easier than expected, a comment from a teacher, an assignment that had some good work in it, noticing that you completed 20 minutes of focused study and it seemed easier and more enjoyable than usual – as you build your study habits over time.

This book started with the idea that life is too good for bad study. I hope you have picked up some ideas as to what good study looks like – ideas like minimising distractions, active approaches, persistence, setting goals, organisation, getting enough sleep, being deliberate with your mindset, working hard in class and starting early on revision and assignment tasks.

I would love you to remember that quote – life is too good for bad study – and, when you sit down to study, study with the intensity you deserve for making the commitment you have.

References

Barton, D. (2016, November 11). 'Three Things Top Performing Students Know That Their Peers Miss'. Retrieved from *Mindshift*: https://www.kqed.org/mindshift/46951/three-things-top-performing-students-know-that-their-peers-miss

Carpenter, S. C. (2012). 'Using Spacing to Enhance Diverse Forms of Learning: Review of Recent Research and Implications for Instruction'. *Educational Psychology Review*, 369–378.

Chunn, L. (2017, May 10). 'The Psychology of the To-do List – Why Your Brain Loves Ordered Tasks'. Retrieved from *The Guardian*: https://www.theguardian.com/lifeandstyle/2017/may/10/the-psychology-of-the-to-do-list-why-your-brain-loves-ordered-tasks

Duckworth, A. (n.d.). 'Grit: The Power of Passion and Perseverance'. (Video). Retrieved from *TED Conferences*: https://www.ted.com/talks/angela_lee_duckworth_grit_the_power_of_passion_and_perseverance?language=en

Dweck, C. (2006). *Mindset: The New Psychology of Success*. New York: Ballentine Books.

Harvard Medical School. (2007). 'Sleep, Learning and Memory'. Retrieved from Harvard Medical School website: https://healthysleep.med.harvard.edu/healthy/matters/benefits-of-sleep/learning-memory

Jensen, E. &. (2013). *Turnaround Tools for the Teenage Brain: Helping Underperforming Students Become Lifelong Learners*. Wiley.

Locke, E. A. (2002). 'Building a Practically Useful Theory of Goal Setting and Task Motivation: A 35-Year Odyssey'. *American Psychologist*, 705–717.

Masicampo, E. J., & Baumeister, R. F. (2011). 'Consider It Done! Plan Making Can Eliminate the Cognitive Effects of Unfulfilled Goals'. *Journal of Personality and Social Psychology*, 667–683.

Rosen, L. D. (2017, October 1). 'The Distracted Student Mind – Enhancing Its Focus and Attention'. Retrieved from *Kappan*: https://kappanonline.org/rosen-distracted-student-mind-attention/

Ryback, R. (2016, October 3). 'The Science of Accomplishing Your Goals'. Retrieved from *Psychology Today*: https://www.psychologytoday.com/au/blog/the-truisms-wellness/201610/the-science-accomplishing-your-goals#:~:text=This%20is%20one%20reason%20people,to%20repeat%20the%20associated%20behavior.

VicHealth. (2017). *Sleep and Mental Wellbeing: Exploring the Links*. Retrieved from VicHealth website.

www.ingramcontent.com/pod-product-compliance
Lightning Source LLC
Chambersburg PA
CBHW050259120526
44590CB00016B/2409